23660

ALL ABOARD AMERICA

Grand Canyon

A Buddy Book
by
Julie Murray

ABDO
Publishing Company

VISIT US AT
www.abdopub.com

Published by ABDO Publishing Company, 4940 Viking Drive, Edina, Minnesota 55435.

Copyright © 2005 by Abdo Consulting Group, Inc. International copyrights reserved in all countries. No part of this book may be reproduced in any form without written permission from the publisher. Buddy Books™ is a trademark and logo of ABDO Publishing Company.

Printed in the United States.

Edited by: Christy DeVillier
Contributing Editors: Michael P. Goecke, Sarah Tieck
Graphic Design: Deborah Coldiron
Image Research: Deborah Coldiron
Photographs: Corel, Leeson Photography, North Wind Pictures, Photodisc

Library of Congress Cataloging-in-Publication Data

Murray, Julie, 1969-
  Grand Canyon / Julie Murray.
        p. cm. — (All aboard America)
  Includes index.
  Summary: An introduction to Arizona's Grand Canyon, one of the Natural Wonders of the World, including how it was formed, who lives nearby, and animals and plants of the region.
  ISBN 1-59197-505-0
    1. Grand Canyon (Ariz.)—Juvenile literature. 2. Grand Canyon National Park (Ariz.)—Juvenile literature. [1. Grand Canyon (Ariz.) 2. Grand Canyon National Park (Ariz.) 3. National parks and reserves.] I. Title.
F788.M895 2004
979.1'32—dc21

23660

                                        2003052258

Table Of Contents

CHAPTER 1

Beautiful Canyon

The Grand Canyon is one of the largest canyons in the world. It is 277 miles (446 km) long and about one mile (two km) deep. At the bottom of the canyon is the Colorado River. People from all over the world visit the Grand Canyon each year.

The Grand Canyon (GRAND CAN-yun)

The Grand Canyon is in northern Arizona. The canyon walls are made of limestone, sandstone, shale, and granite. There are cliffs, caves, **buttes**, and **plateaus**. Visitors can see the canyon's rock layers. At sunset, the canyon walls often look red and orange. It is a beautiful sight.

The Colorado River played an important part in creating the Grand Canyon. The river water ran over rocks and wore them down. This is called **erosion**. Erosion happens slowly over time. About six million years of erosion created the Grand Canyon.

The Grand Canyon is about six million years old.

The Grand Canyon is famous for its old rocks. Rocks at the top of the canyon are about 250 million years old. The oldest rocks are at the bottom of the canyon. They are more than one billion years old.

Long ago, oceans and seas lay where the Grand Canyon stands today. Sharks, sea urchins, snails, clams, and trilobites lived there. Trilobites are sea animals that died out 250 million years ago. **Fossils** of trilobites and other sea animals are common at the Grand Canyon.

A trilobite fossil

People have been living at the Grand Canyon for thousands of years. One group of Native Americans lived there about 4,000 years ago. Scientists call them the Desert Archaic people. Their drawings are still around today. These drawings are called **pictographs**. The Desert Archaic people also made things from twigs. They left behind split-twig figures of different animals.

Pictographs are very old drawings on rock walls.

About 1,000 years ago, the Anasazi people lived at the Grand Canyon. These Native Americans grew their own food. The Anasazi lived in **adobe** homes. **Ruins** of these adobe homes are around today.

Anasazi ruins

The Havasupai have lived at the Grand Canyon for hundreds of years. They live in the Supai village. People cannot reach Supai by car. Visitors must ride a horse or hike.

Many people enjoy hiking to the Supai village.

In 1540, Europeans discovered the Grand Canyon. It was a group of Spanish explorers led by García López de Cárdenas.

In 1869, a famous **expedition** took place. Major John Wesley Powell and his crew explored the Colorado River. It was a dangerous trip through the canyon on the Colorado River. On this trip, Major Powell named the Grand Canyon.

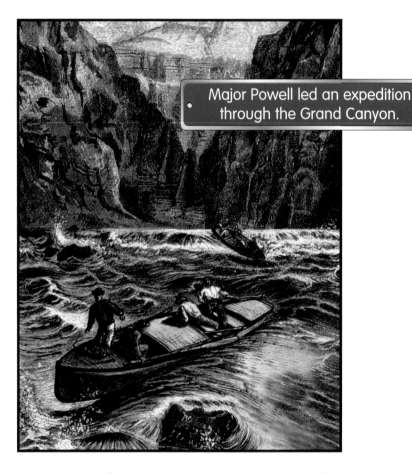

Major Powell led an expedition through the Grand Canyon.

Over the years, more and more people visited the Grand Canyon. People built hotels and restaurants nearby. In 1919, the Grand Canyon became a national park.

The Grand Canyon National Park covers almost 2,000 square miles (5,180 sq km). It is open all year long.

Grand Canyon National Park seen from the South Rim.

Visitors often go to the Grand Canyon's South Rim. This area is dry and desert-like. It is hot in the summer. Hiking along the canyon rim offers great views.

The South Rim is also home to the Grand Canyon Village. This village is full of restaurants, shops, museums, lodges, and campgrounds.

The North Rim is open from mid-May through mid-October. This area has more green plants and shrubs. The weather is cooler and wetter at the North Rim. It gets snow in the winter, too.

The North Rim in the winter.

Many people enjoy hiking down to the Inner Canyon. It is much warmer at the bottom of the canyon. A trip to the bottom and back takes two or three days. People also ride mules down to the Inner Canyon.

Mule rides to the Inner Canyon are common.

Detour ⬇

Did You Know?

Many kinds of animals live at the Grand Canyon. There are bald eagles, rattlesnakes, and mule deer. Kaibab squirrels live in the ponderosa pine trees at the North Rim. They do not live anywhere else in the world.

A Kaibab Squirrel

CHAPTER 6

The Grand Canyon Today

The Grand Canyon is a great place to enjoy the outdoors. There are miles and miles of hiking trails. Some visitors go on long camping trips. Others go boating down the Colorado River. Some people take helicopter rides over the canyon. Bus tours and biking are also common.

Some people enjoy kayaking through the Grand Canyon.

The park also offers special programs for adults and children. Visitors can learn about the canyon's history, **fossils**, animals, and plants.

More than five million people visit the Grand Canyon each year. It is one of the most beautiful places in North America.

Important Words

adobe (uh-DOH-bee) a kind of clay brick.

butte (BYOOT) a hill or mountain with steep sides and a flat top.

erosion (ih-ROH-zhun) wearing away of the land often caused by water or wind.

expedition (ek-spuh-DISH-un) an important trip that may be for exploration.

fossil (fah-suhll) remains of very old animals and plants.

pictograph (PIK-tuh-graff) a very old drawing or painting on a rock wall.

plateau (pla-TOH) high, flat land.

ruins (ROO-uhnz) the damaged remains of a very old building or city.

Web Sites

Would you like to learn more about the Grand Canyon?

Please visit ABDO Publishing Company on the information superhighway to find Web site links about the Grand Canyon. These links are routinely monitored and updated to provide the most current information available.

www.abdopub.com

Index